Parenting Through Grief

JADE RICHARDSON BOCK
CRAIG PIERCE PH.D.

SECOND EDITION

ISBN: 9781695869042

This book is dedicated to the families who shared their stories,
and to hundreds more who give and receive support
at the Children's Grief Center of New Mexico.

childrensgrief.org

ACKNOWLEDGEMENTS

This book is a collection of stories and wisdom gathered over many years from families like yours and mine—families shaped by the loss of a loved one. Like all of the strongest kinds of help, it comes from many hands and hearts.

Greatest of thanks go to the following men and women, who deserve very special recognition: Kelly Geib-Eckenroth and Barbara Fries, LPCC are program coordinators at the Children's Grief Center. They contributed beautiful stories, advice and experience to these pages. Courtney Custer and Nathan Hoge of Southwest Family Guidance Center participated in the nuts and bolts planning and final execution of the book's production. Dr. Craig Pierce, founder of Southwest Family Guidance Center and the Thriving Kids programs, is a visionary, wise counselor, and a fully grown bereaved child who made this project possible with numerous contributions of talent and treasure.

Warmly,

Jade Richardson Bock

CONTENTS

NOTES

Talking To Children About Death

MYTH

Children are fragile and can't handle the truth about death.

FACT

Children are resilient. With honesty and compassion,
they can handle the truth about death.

When is Daddy coming back from heaven?

Annie was distraught. She was worried she had said something terrible to her five-year-old son, something that could not be undone and would confuse and hurt him deeply. "Two weeks ago, my husband passed away. He had been sick for nearly a year—colon cancer. Hospice was wonderful. He died at home, the way he wanted. But last night our son crawled into bed with me and asked 'When is Daddy coming back from heaven?' I panicked! I didn't know what to say. I told him, 'I don't know son. I hope soon.' I couldn't break his heart again. What could I have done differently?"

There aren't any chapters in <u>What to Expect When You're Expecting</u> that cover telling children that their parent has died. We aren't given this information, because we don't typically need it in the normal course of our lives. About 1 in 9 Americans experience the death of a parent before age 20. 1 in 7 lose a parent or sibling. That means about 90% of America's youth do not experience the death of a loved one. The world is geared towards that 90%.

Annie loved her son deeply, yet her heart was battered. She didn't want to cause him any more pain. She thought the truth—daddy is never coming home again—would hurt him more than he could bear. She chose to obscure the truth, just for a little while, until he's old enough to handle it. Annie is not alone in feeling this way; many parents have been in the same situation. Unfortunately, the impulse to try and make hard news easier typically backfires. Children grow and eventually learn that what we told them wasn't true. If that happens, we risk compromising their trust. We also risk compromising the sense of safety we worked hard to cultivate for the children in our care.

Explaining A Death That Has Occurred

Because parents love their kids, it is natural to want to protect them from the pain of loss. However, everyone does better when trusted with the truth. What children imagine can be far worse than the reality they're facing. That's why simplicity and honesty are best.

- Give concrete, clear explanations. Refrain from phrases like "passed away" or "gone to heaven." It is important that children understand that death is permanent, that a person who has died no longer can feel or think, and that they won't be able to come back. "Daddy's cancer got so serious that his body was not able to heal. His heart stopped beating, he stopped breathing. He died."

- Answer only direct questions. Do not give more information than is asked. Children will come back with more questions after they process what you have already said.

- Remind children that death is not their fault. Children tend to be egocentric. As a result, it is important that you help them to understand that they did not cause the loved one to die.

- Once children begin to understand the permanence of death, then you can introduce them to your family's beliefs about the afterlife, if you so choose.

By the Ages

Little Ones (3–6) may worry that their loved one who is buried in a graveyard gets wet when it rains, or is afraid of the dark. Reassure them that when someone dies, they can't experience pain, discomfort, or emotions any longer.

We get into trouble when we start to look for an escape from this hard conversation, and when we fall back on euphemisms like, "he's gone to a better place," or "he's in heaven now." These statements are not reassuring or comforting to young people. When we tell them their loved one is "gone" or "is somewhere else," it sounds like their loved one has left them behind. We need to assure very young children that nothing they did, or didn't do, caused the death.

Very young children may say things like, "My daddy died. Do you know when he's coming home?" This is an opportunity to go back to the beginning and re-explain what death means. Adult caregivers of bereaved children will likely need to have this conversation multiple times.

Older Children (7–12) need reassurance and to hear that their loved one didn't choose to leave. They would be here if they could. Explain that death happens to all of us, and when it occurs, we can't change it.

This age group may be more prone to worries that other people they love will also die. Assure them that most people live for a long time. It's normal for a child to lose a grandparent, because they lived a full lifetime. It's still hard, and we miss them. It's less normal for a child to lose a parent or sibling. Reassure them that it is unlikely they will lose another parent or sibling. Although your loved one has died, you're still a family, and you can get through this together.

At these ages, young people are also likely to create a myth around the death of their loved one: "My mom said my dad had a heart attack, but I think he's really on a secret mission for the CIA, and he's going to come back to us someday." Listen for hints about secret beliefs and gently remind that the person we lost loved us very much, and wouldn't willingly leave us for any reason.

Teens understand that death is permanent and universal, however they are surprisingly prone to believing that they may have caused or could have prevented the death. "If I hadn't slammed my door, he wouldn't have had that heart attack." Just as with very young children, teens need to be reassured that this incident was out of everyone's control.

Teens are in the middle of huge developmental changes. When a death occurs in the family, they often are out of sync with other people's feelings. They want things to stay the same and for their loved ones to "act normally." Sometimes teens take on mannerisms or habits of the deceased, trying to fill their role in the family. Dressing, talking, walking, behaving in ways similar to the person who died is not unusual, and is part of the teen's process of coming to terms with a great loss.

.

Explaining Terminal Illness Or Imminent Death

Most children become aware of death early on. They hear about it in fairy tales, see it in movies, or experience it with the loss of a pet. Death can be one of the hardest subjects to talk about with kids, probably because most adults are uncomfortable with death or are struggling with their own sorrow. Trust that your children have the capacity to deal with the sad truth and handle it in their own way.

If you have not told your children that a loved one is dying, they probably know something is happening , even if no one says it out loud. Body language, worried looks, hushed discussions, telephone calls, relatives showing up, and the general sadness and tension in the adults around them give kids clues that whatever is happening is serious.

- Don't hold back important information. It is important to let children know that a loved one is seriously ill and may die. If the person dies and they are not told, they are unprepared. Because younger children are egocentric, it is important to reassure them that nothing they did or said caused the death.

- Children need honest and correct information in a language they can understand. For example, "Daddy is in the hospital because he is sick with cancer. It is nobody's fault. It is a different kind of sick than a cold or flu. You cannot get it from him. You can still hug and kiss him." Ask children to repeat back what you said so you can be sure that they understand, and invite them to ask questions. Knowing that they will be kept informed about things that are happening will lessen their anxiety.

- Children still need consistent guidance and boundaries. Children need parents to set limits. When parents are in shock and grieving, setting limits can be hard. Others may say, "Oh, let it go. Her mom is dying." Maintaining boundaries, keeping routines in place and household rules intact help kids to feel safe. Without these limits, children feel things are out of control, which can make them feel insecure. Try to keep the schedule as normal as possible.

Visiting The Seriously Ill

Visiting someone who is very sick can be traumatic, especially if children are not prepared in advance.

- **Ask first.** Before you take your children to visit someone who is sick or dying, ask them if they would like to go with you. If the answer is no, ask why. Once the matter is discussed, children will usually opt to go along.

- **Set expectations.** Let children know in advance what the person will look like, what the machines in the room are for, what the room will smell like. Let them know if it's ok to touch or hug the person. You can suggest bringing a gift for the person or have them draw a picture or write a letter.

- **Measure time.** The visit should be relatively short. Ten to twenty minutes is long enough for a child of any age. Make time to talk after the visit so you can address any fears or concerns your children may have. The most important reason for letting them visit is giving them a chance to say goodbye.

By The Ages

At every age and stage, young people need a compassionate adult's guidance in accomplishing William Worden's first "task of grief," to understand what has happened.

For young children, this understanding starts with the fundamental difference between alive and dead.

For older children, it continues with understanding how the loss of their loved one impacts others in their family.

For teens and young adults, significant life milestones (learning to drive, going on a date, graduating, starting college, getting married, having children) are forever altered by the fact that someone they love is missing from these important events.

Everyone in the family is hurting and coming to terms with that hurt in their own way. Adult caregivers, while experiencing their own grief, can create an atmosphere where it's ok to talk about the person who died, share stories, wonder "what if" together, and show emotion. For younger children, those emotions may come and go like clouds passing over the sun. For older teens and young adults, those emotions may feel overwhelming. Regardless of the ages and stages of the young people in your family, know that they can handle the truth. Each of you will get through this journey in your own time and own way, but always together.

Tune In To What Matters Most

RIGHT THING

- It can be difficult to know how to help your children cope with the loss, particularly if you're also working through grief of your own. To help you focus on the right thing, begin by asking yourself a simple question: "Right now, what's most important for my kids?"

RIGHT TIME

- Teach your children about death as soon as possible. It is truly a part of life. Animals, insects, pets, neighbors may die. Take the opportunity to explain the difference between alive and dead.

- If you are anticipating a loved one's death, talk with your children about what they can expect. Don't hold back important information. Be honest and use language they can understand.

RIGHT WAY

- A child should always hear the news of a death from a family member with whom he or she has a close, loving relationship. It's best that this talk take place in a familiar setting, preferably at home.

- Be honest and encourage questions.

NOTES

Call Me If There's Anything I Can Do

Myth

Offering to help with *anything* is what people in crisis need to hear.

Fact

When we're in crisis, we can't figure out exactly what we need,
and often can't take advantage of help when it's offered.

When someone we love dies, friends and family often step forward and offer help. "Call me if there's anything I can do," is a common refrain.

As grieving adults, we often have a difficult time organizing things and making decisions. Your world is turned upside down, and it's hard to know what to do, or where you actually need help. As a result, we don't know how to ask for help and we often don't call our would-be helpers. This furthers our own sense of isolation and feelings of being overwhelmed.

Sometimes our friends flee the scene. Many grieving people report coming out of the shock and haze after the loss and realizing that their friends have seemingly moved on with their lives, leaving the grievers behind. This is another loss.

Jessica's Story

"My husband, Rob, took his life. His mother found him. When his brother called us, I knew the minute I answered the phone that something awful had happened. Rob had been in a very bad place emotionally and had threatened suicide for 18 months. We had gone to several therapists and tried marriage counseling. We couldn't seem to get him the help he needed. I talked to my closest friends about my fears that Rob would hurt himself. They dismissed my concerns by saying he loved us too much to do that. He did love us, and I believe he thought he was sparing us pain by removing himself. We have two sons. Austin had just turned 5, Clay was 2 ½.

Friends and family were there for us that first week. There were things they could do, like making phone calls, food, and plans for a service. My closest friends came together and cleaned my house. The Tuesday after Rob died, I went back to work. I had to work, not only for the income, but for my sanity. I thought getting back to a routine would help me and my sons. That morning my best friend called me at work to check on me. I didn't hear from her again for 11 months.

I honestly think that when someone dies, most people don't know how to respond. At the time, I was resentful, angry, and really hurt. I couldn't understand their behavior. I felt like I had lost not just my husband, but also my best friends. At the Grief Center, I met another parent with a similar experience. He said that other people just don't know what to say or do. I also believe our friends felt a great deal of guilt over Rob's death, the same survivor's guilt that I felt.

I did not know what I needed. People I thought were my friends didn't answer my calls for help. They didn't want to touch my pain. I was stuck in all of these losses for so long. Hearing that other people had lost friends after a death in the family allowed me to make some sense of what was happening, and to understand it wasn't my fault. I ran into my best friend 11 months after she called me at work. I could see that she was uncomfortable. Instead of being angry, I felt compassion for her.

Writing helped me to process these losses. There are places where you struggle to understand. I needed to talk about what the kids and I were going through. Writing helped me to put those thoughts in order and to process them. I connected with other widows on internet forums. I was careful not to spend too much time in those forums, it can become consuming, but I did make some friendships that were helpful.

I still don't have a lot of people around me to talk to. I have reached out in the ways I know how. I often post on social media thoughts that start with 'just for today.' These are my thoughts about Rob, his death, and what our family is going through. People who want to comment or connect often do, and they are very kind and supportive. Those who can't handle it don't, and that's ok. I don't want to forget those turning points. After you lose someone you love, you are not the same person. Your priorities shift. You see the world with different eyes. I don't want to lose that experience. Otherwise, what was the point of going through this pain?"

Don't Let Grief Isolate You

In the beginning, you may not understand that a lot of people can't tolerate the pain you and your children are in. You may have a feeling of, or actually are, abandoned by people in your life. It can be difficult to understand that people may avoid you simply because they are fearful of the pain you are experiencing. They may be so worried that something tragic could happen to them, as unrealistic as that is, that they avoid you. You may feel like saying, "Hey, my situation isn't contagious! Where did everybody go?!"

In your mind, try making it ok that some people can't tolerate the pain. Maybe you'd be the same way if it was reversed. Who knows?

The key is to surround yourself with people who make you feel heard and supported. Maybe you can even try humor with a friend and say, "I promise I won't have a meltdown if you come over, I just really need help getting my kids' rooms organized!" The point is, tell people exactly what you need and, if you can, let them know that sometimes all you need is logistical support, not emotional support. Let your guard down and accept offers of help.

Remember, you can say, "I don't know what I need right now, ask me again." It can often be six or more months after the death that you realize what you need.

Be Specific About What You Need

In the haze of grief it's hard to know what you need. That can make it even more difficult to ask for help. Take heart, over time you will learn to ask for and get the help required.

Suggestion: Posting on social media a specific request can make it easier for people to enter your lives and give what help they can. "Can someone give me some ideas on how to fix my dishwasher?" might work. A word of caution: sometimes requests for help go unanswered. We must learn to be ok without it.

Support For Your Children

As a parent, you still have to be attuned to what your kids need. They have their own grief to process. They need normalcy. They need routine and fun. You may feel that you just can't do it all. When that happens, try calling a family member or close friend and asking them to help make sure you're not missing something important.

Grief impacts how your brain functions, so you will miss details! Your sister may tell you your kids could use some new clothes. If you don't have the energy to go to shopping, ask for help. Most people in your life would be so willing to provide assistance, if they knew what to do. Don't be the person that says, "No, no, I'm fine. I can take care of it." Let them help you. Call your sister or friend and say, "Can you please take the kids shopping for winter coats and some new shoes?" Chances are they will jump at the chance to contribute.

Tune In To What Matters Most

RIGHT THING

- When a loved one dies, it often feels like the world has been turned upside down. You might feel out of sync, like your mind is disorganized and no longer working correctly. You're right. You are in the fog of grief and your mind isn't operating in its usual way, and that's ok. The key is to name and normalize what you are experiencing so you can communicate feelings and needs with others.

- Your friends and loved ones have no clue about how you feel, what you think, what you need, or what you want. The only solution is to tell them.

RIGHT TIME

- When is the right time to engage the help of others?
  The sooner the better.

- Put a support system in place as quickly as you can. Enlist friends and loved ones to pick up groceries, run errands, bring food, help with house or yardwork, take the children to the zoo so you can have some alone time, or something as simple as driving you to a support group meeting. Getting help with these practical tasks can lift an enormous weight off your shoulders.

RIGHT WAY

- While your friends and loved ones can't take away the pain of loss, they can provide much needed comfort and support. Let them.

- Look for opportunities to call on another's assistance. Get a loved one to help you create a list of tasks you need help with.

- When the next person says, "Call me if there is anything I can do," let them know what you need, and be specific. We all handle tasks better when they are clearly defined.

- If you're not sure what you need at that moment, say something like: "I appreciate your support, but right now I just don't know what I need. I know I will need some help in the future. May I call you then?"

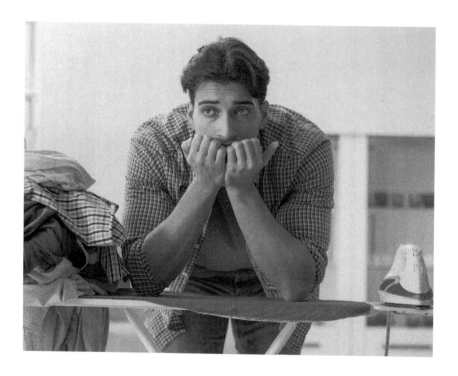

NOTES

Going Back To School After A Death In The Family

Myth
School staff are experts in working with children, even children in crisis.

Fact
Childhood bereavement is not addressed
in most education and counseling programs.

Maribel's Story

"My son Santiago was barely five when his father died. He had a heart attack one night in his sleep. Santiago came into our bedroom and saw me crying and doing CPR. He watched the ambulance take his father's body away. It was so hard on all of us. When kindergarten started that fall, I told his teachers and the school counselor what he had been through. Santiago was a handful. He was angry, sad, and confused. He didn't know where his daddy had gone, or why his mother was sad all the time.

For Christmas, the teacher had the students write letters to Santa asking for presents. Santiago asked for his daddy to come back. The teacher sent him to the counselor. The counselor basically told him he had to write the letter asking for something he could actually have, and had him redo the assignment. I was so disappointed in the school for handling a child's grief in such a thoughtless manner. Santiago's pain wasn't respected."

The death of a parent, grandparent, sibling, or other loved one can throw a child into a confusing tailspin. The child's feelings can bounce from sadness to anger to guilt and back all in a matter of hours. For parents and caregivers, returning to a regular routine is an important part of helping a child find their way in this new landscape shaped by loss.

One of the many issues parents struggle with is how to ease a bereaved child back into school. When should the child return? How much should the parent tell the teacher? Who should tell the classmates? Sometimes these questions can create friction between kids and their guardians. Older children and teens may say they don't want anyone at school to know about the death. Often, they want one place in their lives where they don't have talk about the loss.

A young tween at the Children's Grief Center lost his mother to breast cancer. He wanted school to be a place where "things were normal," and begged his grandparents not to tell the new middle school about his mother's death. The school year progressed without incident until May. One of his teachers had the class work on Mother's Day cards. Facing his first Mother's Day without his mom was hard enough. Now he was in a quandary. He made the card. But then he took it to the bathroom and tore it into little pieces. His heart was broken, and he was filled with rage. That night he attended his support group at the Grief Center and said, "Those teachers are so stupid! How could they make us do that?"

A young person's desire to fly under the school's radar is understandable, especially when it comes to talking about death.

Even well-intentioned adults can be susceptible to saying or doing insensitive things. We strongly advocate that the adult guardian have a face-to-face visit with the child's teachers and school counselor to explain what has happened, and what the student's wishes are.

Not every school has the resources to appropriately support the loss of a student's parent or sibling. It's ok to suggest resources, ask questions, and be part of making a plan. Should the teacher announce the death in the class before the student returns and suggest ways classmates could be supportive? Can the counselor or supportive staff offer the student an open-door policy if they need to talk or just get away? Can academic expectations be adjusted for a time? Does the school staff have experience in helping students cope with a death, or do they need to reach out to a place like the Children's Grief Center to learn effective tools?

The most important thing you can do is ensure the school staff know about the death. This is the best chance your children will have to receive the support, compassion and understanding they need at school. To provide this, you must communicate with your child's teachers and school counselor.

It is important to realize that communication with our bereaved children is just as important as the communication with school officials. Discussing their preferences about informing the school is a good starting point. It is understandable that they may request you tell the school nothing. Many children want the school environment to be a safe haven. They want a place where they don't have to think or talk about their loss, a place where no one sees them in a different light, where they are not treated differently because they are grieving. Just as adults often see work as a place for normalcy, children can see school in a similar light, a place where things can be the way they used to be.

If your children ask you to not say anything to the school, find out why. Once you understand their fears and concerns, you'll be able to calm their apprehensions. For example, if they are afraid peers will find out and they don't want to be pitied or alienated, you can incorporate safeguards. In this instance, you might want to only inform the teachers they interact with and school counselors. Let them know that you do not want classmates informed and to address the subject when absolutely necessary, if privacy can be assured. Including your children in this process can be empowering to them, and can help ease their anxieties.

Acting quickly is critical. It is generally helpful for kids to return to school soon after the death of a family member. If they are in the middle of the school year when their loved one dies, time is of the essence. Addressing the loss, and how to handle its effects in the school setting, needs to happen as soon as possible. If the loss happens during the summer, you have a little extra time to prepare your children and the school.

Tackling the issue of school in a timely way will help ensure that your child has the understanding and appropriate support of the school staff. It will also help your child to transition back to friends and academics more smoothly. The longer the school is uninformed, the longer your children will have to navigate their grief alone. This could result in unintentional, unfortunate mishandling of any atypical behaviors triggered by grief. Coming up with a plan with your children, and setting it in motion quickly, is the best way to help them navigate the difficult path of grief in a school setting.

Some schools are better equipped than others to help grieving children transition back to school. Even if your school doesn't offer specific services, reaching out to the principal, teachers, and the school counselor can give your children the best chance at a successful transition back to school, and a loving start to healing. Informing the staff of your child's loss will help to avoid misunderstandings and insensitive comments. Even so, expect children to have difficult times, regardless of our careful planning.

The loss of a loved one can feel like the end of the world. If at any point you feel the school and/or their staff is not equipped to compassionately accommodate your grieving children and their needs, it can be a good idea to reach out to professional grief centers. Grief centers can often help schools to understand and appropriately handle bereaved children.

The national center locator at childrengrieve.org will tell you if there is a grief support program in your community.

RIGHT THING

- Make a plan. Involve your children in preparing for the return to school. Listen carefully to their needs and wants so that you can effectively communicate those desires to school administrators.

- Talk to the school. Make an appointment with the school principal, teachers, and counselors to discuss your children's needs and wishes. Allowing your children to be present at this meeting can be a good idea. Some children will want to be a part of this to ensure the plan they agreed upon is communicated to their satisfaction. This can create a sense of ease. Other children will not want to be a part of this process, in which case, it is perfectly appropriate for them to entrust communication to you.

- Brainstorm coping skills for when things are tough. Your children will inevitably have some tough moments or days at school. Spend some time talking with them about things they can do to cope when they are having a hard time. This may mean talking to a special friend or trusted teacher at school, carrying something with them that helps them feel comforted or safe, or asking for time to go to the school counselor. To help make this easier, consider coming up with a signal or phrase your children can use when they feel the need to be dismissed from the classroom. Setting up a predetermined key phrase or signal for them to use with teachers, or allowing them to call you from school, can help reduce their stress and facilitate their immediate needs.

RIGHT TIME

- Collaborate with the school as quickly as possible for the best result. Ask school staff for suggestions on how best to reintegrate into the classroom. Do they advise that your children return to school full-time, or would it be better to return for just a few hours a day at first, gradually working toward full days? Can your children be given a break in the counselor's office after being in class for a couple hours as a way to rest and regroup? Sorting out these details early will save added stress for you and your child later on.

- Think ahead. Work with the school to address upcoming lessons and events that may be difficult. As we saw in the earlier example, a simple heads-up about making Mother's Day cards in class would have given the tween's guardian a chance to prepare for this upcoming activity or make alternative plans.

RIGHT WAY

- Encourage teachers to prepare. If your child is okay with classmates knowing about their loss, encourage teachers to talk to students about what to say and what not to say, before your kid returns. Similarly, talk with your child about what they may want to tell classmates. Some children want to tell everyone; others don't. It's important to let children say as much or as little as they want. If your child is uncomfortable discussing the death with other kids, help them practice something they can say if questions arise, and how to talk with teachers if other children keep asking them uncomfortable questions.

- Make a communication plan. Encourage teachers to share their observations. Knowing as soon as possible about any changes in behavior or performance can help you redirect your children and provide extra support, if needed. If it's a new school year, your children's teachers may not yet know them. In this case you can encourage them to speak with last year's teachers to get a sense of how your children typically behave and interact. It will be important that you, the teachers, and school counselors stay in contact in a way that works for all parties. Determine how often and in what way to keep in touch, such as through a weekly email or a call every few weeks.

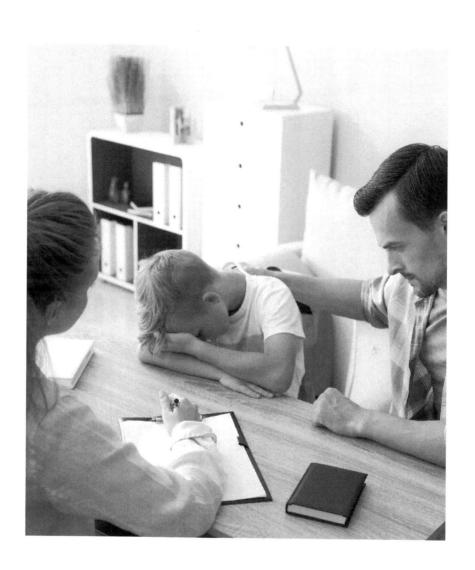

NOTES

What If The Kids See Me Crying?

Myth
It's bad if the kids see me crying; they need me to be strong.

Fact
Kids need consistency and safety but they also need honesty.
It's ok if we show our emotions and share that we too
are missing the person who died.

Rebecca & Frank's Story

Our grandson Christian was 18 months old when his father, our son, died suddenly. He was only 26 years old. Christian lived with his mother but would spend weekends and special times with us. When he was old enough to talk, we started telling him stories about his father and showing him pictures, especially pictures of the two of them together. We told Christian his father was in heaven, and watching over him.

One day we were talking with an old friend, someone we respect a great deal and consider to be a wise man. He told us we shouldn't have been showing Christian pictures of his father. He said, "Reminding him of his loss is like continuously ripping the bandaid off the wound—it will never heal." Christian is five years old now, and he says he wishes his daddy was here. Did we do something wrong? Should we have tried to make him forget his father?"

Rebecca and Frank's friend was speaking with compassion, with their best interests in mind. What he was saying makes a lot of sense from a logical standpoint. However, Christian's heart is not ruled by logic. He is a little boy who needs to understand where he came from, and what has changed in his family.

By learning about his father, Christian will learn about himself. By sharing their love and grief over the loss of their son, Rebecca and Frank will forge a stronger connection with their grandson. In showing Christian that it hurts when we lose someone we love, but we can remember him by telling stories, his grandparents are modeling healthy grieving behaviors, which is just what Christian needs.

Family is usually our best support system when we experience something difficult. When someone in the family dies, everyone's understanding and coping skill are different. This can turn family members away from each other, creating more stress, more loss, and can splinter the family apart. Spending time together can remind family members of the person who is missing, and we're not sure how to deal with the pain of that loss.

Siblings may fight amongst themselves. "You're crying all the time! Dad wouldn't have wanted that!" Or, "You're acting like nothing happened! Going on like our father didn't die. That's disrespecting his memory!" Adults and young people may want to talk about the person they lost, but they don't want to see the other person cry. They change the subject, leave the house, or pick a fight.

Teenagers will often carry on like the death didn't occur, or conversely, try to fill the role of the deceased person in the family taking on their responsibilities or mannerisms. Adults are often in shock, then deeply grieving, finding it difficult to make everyday decisions or even remember where they put their car keys! Very young children don't really understand what has happened to their loved one. Everyone in the family is hurting, and expressing it in different ways.

It's ok if the kids see you crying. It's ok to say, "I really miss daddy. This isn't your fault, and I don't want you to be worried for me. Of course we're all sad, and sometimes we cry."

Always tell the truth in age-appropriate doses. The little one who asked, "When is daddy coming back from heaven?" needs to know that death is permanent, and that no one, no matter how much we loved them or they loved us, can come back to life after dying. To very young children we can explain the death in concrete terms, "His heart isn't beating anymore. He's not breathing anymore. He has died. He can't feel, or think, or laugh, or cry. We can though, and we will miss him very, very much. We can say goodbye."

Be prepared to re-explain and discuss the death (what happened, how it happened) as the child grows and matures. As Fred Rogers said, "If it's mentionable, it's manageable." You can manage having these hard conversations in your family. With practice, it gets easier.

What we don't tell them, they will tell themselves—and often the story they make up is far worse than the truth. If we don't explain to them in simple, concrete terms the facts of the situation, and especially that the death was beyond anyone's control and not anyone's fault, they may think it's somehow their fault that their person died. Even teenagers need to be explicitly told, "This was not your fault." Often, we want to find someone to blame—the doctors, the ambulance driver, even the person who died, but we must remind ourselves and each other that bad things just happen. It's not fair, and it's not right. Our work is to learn how to cope with that, and ultimately to reinvest in life.

Taking Care

In times of stress, it's typical to put ourselves at the bottom of the "to-do list." However, as flight attendants tell us, we must put on our own oxygen mask before helping others. Move your needs up on the list. Take some time to care for yourself, and acknowledge that you are beginning a very difficult, life-changing journey.

Start a conversation with other family members about how each person will care for themselves. Purposely schedule healthy activities that you and your kids will enjoy. This is part of your work.

The death of someone we love changes us forever. It is one of the hardest things we'll ever face in our lives. We must be gentle with ourselves, and our loved ones, as we venture into a new way of being— living with loss.

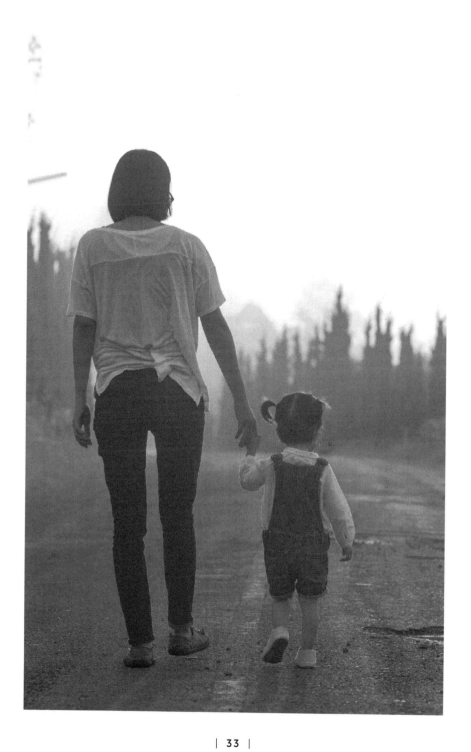

Tune In To What Matters Most

RIGHT THING

- Start by tuning in to how you're taking care of yourself. Try to take a few minutes each day, or even a few hours, to pay attention to how you are feeling and what you can do to nurture yourself.

- Exercising, drinking plenty of water, and eating well are more important when your body and mind are under stress than any other time. Set aside time to do these things for yourself, a little every day.

- Work on accepting your feelings, whatever they may be, and allow yourself to grieve. Sadness, loneliness, fear, confusion and anger—these painful emotions are a natural and normal response to loss. You can try and suppress them or hide from them, but in the end ignoring your feelings will only prolong the grieving process. By tuning in and acknowledging your pain and taking responsibility for your feelings, you can help avoid the complications that often come with unresolved grief, such as depression, anxiety, substance abuse and health problems.

RIGHT TIME

- Give yourself permission to let emotions come and go. It's okay to be angry, to go to an open field and yell, to cry, or to not cry. At the same time, it's also okay to laugh and to find moments of joy.

- Remain open to taking in the pain and meaning of death a little at a time. Your grief is your own, and no one has the right to tell you when you should be "over it," or when to "move on." Grief takes as long as it takes to resolve itself. It is an intensely personal process that can't be measured by a formula or timetable.

RIGHT WAY

- One of the most effective ways to express grief is through some tangible or creative expression of your emotions. Try journaling, writing a letter that expresses the feelings you wish you had shared with your loved one, creating artwork that celebrates the person's life or depicting what you lost.

- Set aside time to do things that make you feel good or are comforting, like taking a hot bath, listening to music, or hiking.

- Learn to accept that grief is hard work. It consumes a lot of energy and can be exhausting. For this reason, it's important to remember that you can reach out for help. Allowing others to be of assistance, and to love you through this challenging time, is a key to healing.

- If at any time the grief feels too much for you to bear, seek guidance from a professional therapist. They can help you and your family take the next steps along the path of living and parenting through grief.

NOTES

CHAPTER 5
Coping With Fears

Myth

Kids are happy-go-lucky and don't worry about the future like adults.

Fact

After a loved one has died, kids typically worry a
similar tragedy will befall someone else close to them.

The unthinkable has happened, and a loved one is gone. Once the shock wears off, and understanding that death is permanent sets in, we often experience new fears. We learn that our world is much more out of our control than we would like. Accidents happen. Doctors can't cure all diseases. People hurt other people. Suddenly, life can be very scary.

William Worden, author of the Childhood Bereavement Project, followed 70 families with 125 children between the ages of 6–12 who experienced the death of a parent. He found that four months after the death, 44% of the children reported their greatest fear is that the other parent will die. A year after the death of a parent, 62% of the children were worried for their other parent.

At the Grief Center, we often do activities around sharing fears. One is called The Worry Tree. Nearly all children write that they are afraid of losing the other parent. They often have day dreams about what could happen to cause their remaining loved ones' deaths. Yet, they typically don't share these worries with their caregivers for fear of upsetting them, or causing more strife in the family. Regardless of what fears they do or don't express, the young people in your family need to know that there is a plan in place to care for them.

Adults have fears, too. They find it scary to plan for the future after a spouse or child has died. Everything is different now. Our assumptions about how life will be have forever changed. No one can promise to "always be there," we know it isn't true. Help your children understand that their fears are not only ok, they are perfectly normal, and shared by many others who have lost a loved one. Often, kids feel like they are the only ones who have these fears. It can ease their minds to know that other kids have the same scary thoughts.

Putting A Name On Fear

What are some of the fears your children may experience?

- **Fear of losing a parent or other loved ones.** To a child, a parent is everything. When one dies, a child's fear of losing the other parent can become powerful and overwhelming. To deal with the intense fear of being left unprotected and alone, children may act overly needy, never wanting to leave your side. Any time apart can become a source of tremendous anxiety.

- **Fear of abandonment.** The emotional trauma of losing a parent, sibling, relative, or friend can spark intense fears of being left behind and abandoned. They may express fear of everyday events like going to school or the grocery store. Physical symptoms like stomach aches and headaches may surface whenever your children are separated from you and want to return home. Bedwetting, sluggishness, and uncharacteristic forgetfulness may also be signs that your children are dealing with unspoken fears, unresolved grief, and are in need of attention and reassurance.

- **Fear of death.** When a parent or loved one dies, it's not uncommon for children to fear that they too will die soon. A child may wonder, "Grandpa died in his sleep. Am I going to die too when I go to bed tonight?" Death might be linked to a hospital, a car accident, a particular disease; whatever the cause of their loved one's death, they may develop a fear that they will die in the same way.

- **Fear of sleep.** Going to bed can make some children fearful as many equate sleep with death. A child who is afraid to go to sleep may ask to read book after book at night, cry incessantly, or prolong their preparations for bed. The fear of sleep may result in recurring nightmares, which further feed their fear of going to bed at night. As a result, sleep disorders such as insomnia are a common experience for children who lose a loved one.

- **Fear of showing emotions.** While young children typically display their emotions easily in the face of grief, older kids may become afraid to do so out of fear of saying or doing the wrong thing. They may feel guilty for making you cry and/or express anger at others for talking about the person who died. This can make it extremely difficult for a young person to process the powerful and often conflicting emotions of grief.

- **Fear of the unknown.** Death creates unimaginable upheaval in a family's life and the powerful emotions that come with this event can cause children to become afraid of everyday situations and events. Anxiety may set in, along with undefined fears and generalized uneasiness that something terrible is about to happen.

Communication in the family is the key to wiping away worries. Let your kids tell you their fears, and let them know that it's ok to feel scared or to cry. It's ok if you cry when they tell you their fears. It's important for kids to know that they are not adding stress or worry by sharing their thoughts with you. Kids might hesitate to share their feelings unless they know this.

For older kids, share that you worry too, and describe what that feels like. Sometimes sharing our fears is actually comforting, because then we are no longer wondering what our child or parent is thinking. By being honest, you take some of the mystery out of the equation. This is especially important for younger children because their thoughts can run wild, and their imaginings are often far worse than reality.

Calming Fears

One mother shared, "If I am going to be late to pick my kids up, I know they will worry. When that happens, I call the school and insist they tell my children that I called and am on my way." This parent is using communication to alleviate her kids' worry, so they know she is just running late and nothing bad has happened. Another parent said, "The first year after my husband died was the scariest. I was worried about everything. Every phone call made me jump. I needed to know where my kids were at all times. Over time, that began to lessen."

As parents, we know all too well how much we worry about our kids. After the loss of a loved one, that worry can take on a whole new power. This is to be expected, but it won't last forever. Be mindful of what you can do to feel more secure. For example, have your kids call you as soon as they get home if you are not there, or ask the babysitter to call you every couple of hours, just so you know everything is ok.

For many parents, taking action helps. As difficult as it is, you must deal with the issue practically by putting in place a contingency plan for their care. If you do not have a will and life insurance in place, now is the time to do so. If you did have these in place before the loss of a loved one, especially a spouse or a child, they will need to be updated to reflect the family's new situation. Be sure these documents name guardians for the kids, and if you feel your children are old enough, share this information with them so they understand what would happen to them in the event that you are no longer there to care for them. You must be able to tell your kids that there is a plan for their well-being. This will help them feel more at ease, and will relieve pressure. You can feel confident that there is a detailed plan in place should the unthinkable happen.

Tune In To What Matters Most

RIGHT THING

- Take time to tune in to how your children are experiencing the loss. What are they feeling and thinking?

- It is common for children to fear the surviving parent's death. Tune in to this. Fear is a normal response. You can help calm your child's fears once they are identified. Reassuring them that they will always be cared for, and a plan is in place for them, is a concrete way to help allay their fears.

RIGHT TIME

- The time for communication with your children and planning for their safety and care if you were to die unexpectedly is now.

- Let your children know that it always is ok to share their feelings and fears.

- For smaller children or children who aren't very vocal, it is often a good idea to use drawing or writing to help them express what they are feeling and how they are experiencing the death. Picking different colors of crayons, scribbling with different intensities on a piece of paper can help them describe the strong feelings they may have.

- Let them know it is ok to cry, and it is ok to say things that are sad.

RIGHT WAY

- Plan, plan, plan! It is critical to have plans in place for your children if anything were to happen to you.

- Make sure you have updated your will, name one or more guardians to assume responsibility for your children if something were to happen to you, get life insurance if possible, and do it now.

- Take time to share the plan with your children. They need to know that they will always be protected no matter what happens.

NOTES

Secondary Losses

Myth

You don't need to grieve secondary losses because they are insignificant when compared to the loss of a person.

Fact

Secondary losses are real and painful. Just like greiving the person who died, mourning secondary losses allows you to move forward.

Alan's Story

When Alan was 17, his 24 year old sister Ana died by suicide. She was a recent college graduate, a bright, creative, successful, beautiful young woman. "When word got out of her death, many people came to our house. I retreated to watch Harry Potter for 3 days. I didn't want to talk about it—that wasn't what I needed. Ana had attended a prestigious college. I was applying to very competitive schools at the time. I was successful in high school, and appeared to be doing alright.

Almost a year later, I received an online acceptance letter and opened it. I immediately went from being ecstatic to sobbing a minute later. Here was a wonderful thing that I couldn't share with her. She would have been so proud. I printed the letter and took it to the cemetery, to my sister's grave. This was something I needed to do on my own. I know she'll never know my partner, she'll never come to my wedding.

There's a litany of things I'll never get to experience with her.

It wasn't until my sophomore year in college that I wanted to talk about it. I found a counselor through my school to help me process my sister's death. I needed to meet some of my own goals before I was able to deal with the grief."

When Alan lost his sister, her death was stunning. Like most of us, Alan waded through the numbing, heavy feelings of loss. As days and weeks go by, other realizations start to arise. The initial loss is great. We lose our loved one, and someone who loved us back. Then we realize that we have lost the ability to share our special moments, ask them for advice, rely on them for support.

Sometimes we're confronted by the loss surprisingly; in the store we pick up their favorite treat only to be reminded that they aren't here to enjoy it. A simple trip to the grocery suddenly ends up in tears and frustration.

For young people, the impact of secondary losses goes on and on. It's a factor in how kids re-grieve the loss, progressing through developmental stages and gaining new understanding of how the death continues to impact their life. Secondary losses can be a pinprick on the balloon of our special days. They can feel deflating. It can seem as though joyous occasions are clouded by the shadow of loss.

C.S. Lewis, the man who gave us the Chronicles of Narnia, wrote another powerful tale, A Grief Observed. This book describes his experience after losing the great love of his life. "I think I am beginning to understand why grief feels like suspense. It comes from the frustration of so many impulses that had become habitual. Thought after thought, feeling after feeling, action after action, had Helen for their object. Now their target is gone. I keep on through habit fitting an arrow to the string; then I remember and have to lay the bow down."

Examples of Secondary Losses

An 8-year-old boy whose 12-year-old brother was killed asked his mother, "Does this mean I have to do all of his chores?" This boy is not being selfish at all. It is developmentally normal for children to focus on details such as this, and how they will impact them. The truth is, this boy lost a brother, playmate, teammate, and someone who shared the chores. Here are other examples of secondary losses you may encounter:

- **Loss of a role:** "I'm no longer someone's dad, wife, sister, etc."

- **Loss of a family structure:** The family may now have one child/parent instead of two.

- **Loss of financial contribution:** The family now might have to survive on less income.

- **Loss of attention**: Especially for children, if a parent or sibling dies, there is one less person to play with them and take them places.

- **Loss of a special role:** "Dad was the one who played baseball with me and now I can't play baseball anymore."

- **Loss of community:** If the family has to move after a death, everyone in the family loses friends, neighbors, classmates and other important people.

- **Loss of self-efficacy:** You may feel that you have lost the ability to manage daily life, meet your kids' needs and attend to what needs to be done.

- **Loss of a support person:** "Grandma was my go-to person to talk with about friends. Now I don't have that outlet anymore."

- **Loss of logistical support:** If a parent was always the one who took the children to soccer practice and now the other parent has to work full time, there may be no one to take them to practice.

- **Loss of a partner in activities:** "My husband and I played cards on Friday nights with two other couples. I can't do that anymore."

- **Loss of faith, safety, and trust:** Especially when someone dies in a tragic or violent way, we question our faith, our sense of security in the world is broken, and we may find it hard to trust others.

- **Loss of health and wellbeing:** After a loss, health issues are common due to stress, lack of sleep, and emotional trauma.

The key to disarming the impact of secondary losses is to acknowledge them. Try to look at life from your other family member's perspective. How has the loss of the loved one changed the trajectory of your future? This is going to be different for each person in the family. Their relationship with the deceased was unique, and their experience of losing that person will be unique, as well. It's important to recognize that secondary losses are a way of describing the incremental—and sometimes surprisingly painful—ways we miss our loved one. We lived a life together. Secondary losses, in their painful pinpricks and sudden realizations, slowly teach us that we can live that life apart from them.

Tune In To What Matters Most

RIGHT THING

- After the loss of a loved one, try to identify what potential secondary losses exist for you. Do the same for your children. Their secondary losses are likely to be different than your own.

  For example, if your spouse has died, you experience the loss of your love, but also financial losses, the loss of a parenting partner, etc. Your children may be dealing with the loss of someone to care for them and play with them. Talking about secondary losses will help you establish a new normal and adjust to life's differences after a loved one has died.

- Try to minimize the impact of the secondary loss by finding alternatives that could fill that need. For example, if the secondary loss is that dad used to make pancakes every Sunday morning, what new ritual could your family create? Maybe you could still make pancakes on Sundays and talk about dad as you eat breakfast. Or, you could visit their father's grave on Sunday mornings instead. The point is to create new rituals while also acknowledging the pain of the loss of the original ritual or experience. Assess what you want to keep about the ritual and what you want to change, then begin to put the new practice into place.

RIGHT TIME

- For many issues relating to grief, the right time to address them is as soon as possible. When it comes to secondary losses, however, sooner is not always better. Your family needs to feel ready to acknowledge the loss before they can move on to a new tradition or practice.

- Do not try to address every secondary loss at once, deal with them as they arise. Secondary losses you haven't considered will continue to show up days, weeks, months, or even years from now.

- Kids will bring up things the moment they are experiencing them, so as a parent, stop and tune in to your children when they bring up an issue. That is the time to respond.

- Pay attention to when kids resist doing things they once loved to do. They may avoid activities that are too painful after the loss. Be attuned and avoid forcing them to participate in things they resist.

RIGHT WAY

Anticipate that secondary losses will arise and throw you back into the depths of grief, even if you have been feeling better. Anticipate that people around you might be confused by this. You may want to explain to them why you suddenly appear to be acting as you did just after the death occurred, even though it is many months later. If the people around you understand why you are struggling, they may be more likely to offer support, and less likely to withdraw or avoid you. As you move through these losses, be authentic about what feels right for you and your family. Remember, every person and every family handles secondary losses in their own way.

NOTES

NOTES

MILESTONES & HOLIDAYS

Myth

It is important to maintain family traditions,
and keep as much the same as possible.

Fact

It is important to acknowledge that things are not the same, and it's
ok to make changes. Involve the whole family, and acknowledge what
each person wants to keep and what they want to do differently.

Happy Holidays?

Due to the huge emphasis placed on family togetherness during the
holiday season and special days like graduation, birthdays, anniversaries,
etcetera, we become acutely aware of the void in our lives left by loved
ones who have died. There is no right or wrong way for how things
should go during this time, but the more you plan ahead and start
thinking about how to manage the impending celebrations, the easier
it will be. We will be sad at times. We may even dread those special
days we used to enjoy so much. What if this holiday season we made a
little space for that sadness? What if, together, we acknowledged that
someone we loved so much is missing? What if we found a way to
remember that person with honor and warmth? What if, together, we
talked about our special traditions, and made new ones?

Jade's Story

"As I write it's October—the 18th, actually. For me the holiday season begins today with my father's birthday. Next week is the anniversary of his death and a new milestone. I was 17 when he died. That was 18 years ago. He's now been dead for more years than we had together. My father was a commercial pilot and he was killed in a plane crash on October 27th on the small Pacific island of Saipan.

Halloween, a holiday he had already planned his costume for, was spent preparing for his funeral. I still don't remember Thanksgiving that year. I do recall flashes from that first Christmas. It was so empty, sad, and despite Micronesia's tropical climate, it felt cold. My mother made an American treat for Christmas dinner that year—spaghetti. My newly shrunken family ate together in silence, and tried not to make eye contact.

I recently spoke with a grandmother who is raising grieving grandchildren after the death of their mother, her daughter. I asked how she was feeling about all this. With a heavy sigh, she said she doesn't want to cry in front of the children because she doesn't want them to feel sad, and start crying, too. That sounded very familiar to me. "I don't want to appear sad, because I don't want you to feel sad." We're all sad enough on the inside, right? We pretend there are no lumps in our throats or tears in our eyes. I think that's how my family felt, and I think those feelings ultimately had a hand in driving us apart for so many years after my father's sudden death. When we were together, we were unavoidably reminded that Dad was missing—not that we ever truly forgot."

Individuals and families go through myriad emotional, physical, and cognitive reactions during the holidays. They may feel guilt, confusion, anger, or the need to withdraw and isolate themselves. Some people may turn to harmful coping techniques: excessive drinking, drug use, or aggressive and/or reckless behavior. Children are often confused about how celebratory they should feel.

Little children are naturally excited about the holidays, in sharp contrast to older people's sadness. Other reactions include trouble sleeping, changes in appetite, difficulty concentrating, becoming clumsy or forgetful, or even suffering from panic attacks. It is important to recognize that these are normal and common reactions. We need to focus on becoming more aware that we are hurting, and that we need special care during these harder-than-usual times.

The National Alliance for Grieving Children emphasizes the importance of facing the holidays with "intentionality," meaning you are planning for holidays beforehand and developing strategies for coping. By having conversations and making plans early, the emotions and energy surrounding the experience are spread out over a period of time, rather than being concentrated in one day. You may wish to create a new tradition, or stick to things you have done in the past. Remember that whatever you decide to do the first year, you are not obligated to do the next. Helping others in need could be a great way to take your mind off the grief that you are feeling. Another idea is to plan a special celebration. It can be helpful to have something fun to look forward to. If things feel overwhelming, plan to call on all of those people who have said, "If you need anything," and ask them for help.

It is important to try to include the young people in your family in holiday planning as much as possible. Talk about what traditions you want to keep, what you want to change, or what you might try differently just for this year. Assign specific responsibilities to each family member, consider doing a special project together to remember your loved one, and suggest discussion topics to talk about as a family. A list of ideas for activities is at the end of this chapter.

At the Children's Grief Center, one thing we learn is that letting tears fall is actually not the end of the world. Truthfully, the worst has already happened—that's why we're all grieving. Allowing yourself to feel the feelings is ok.

Kids are expert at this. They feel those hard feelings, and then they feel something else. Like a cloud passing over the sun, the pain comes and goes in doses just right for their size. They feel it, they acknowledge it, they go play, and the cycle continues. We could learn much from their bravery. "Going on" doesn't mean we'll forget our special person. We'll never stop loving them or feeling the memory of their love for us, but sometimes we will surprisingly "feel everything becoming alright."

Just as there is no right or wrong way to grieve, there is no right or wrong way to experience special days without our loved one. The key is to genuinely experience them in their imperfection, their pain, and their little surprises.

Tune In To What Matters Most

RIGHT THING

- When it comes to holidays or special days, being prepared to tune in and genuinely acknowledge the feelings and emotions surrounding your family's loss is of utmost importance.

- Processing these emotions and planning for how we want these special days to be celebrated will help minimize the number of unpredictable emotions that can overwhelm us.

- How can you prepare for emotions and reactions that you don't necessarily know are going to manifest? We just have to do the best we can, and believe that will get us through. It is a learning process, it can be certainly be difficult, but with some experience we will get better at navigating these difficult days.

RIGHT TIME

- The sooner you prepare for a holiday or special day the better. Greater preparation will result in fewer difficulties in managing the day. It doesn't guarantee that we won't experience bumps in the road, but it will help minimize the chances we do.

- The reality is that you have probably run into a few challenging moments already, and it is likely that you will still run into more. The encouraging side to this is that each pothole serves as an opportunity to learn and develop your unique approach to navigating difficult times.

- Don't be afraid to try new approaches. Not all of them will work, but discovering what isn't helpful for your family has value as well. Sometimes, knowing what doesn't work can help you discover what does. As Thomas Edison once said: "I learned 10,000 ways not to make a light bulb."

RIGHT WAY

- Having one or more family meetings prior to a holiday can be a helpful way to anticipate potentially difficult situations. Having one meeting a month or so out, and another a couple of days before the holiday, will help you formalize an effective strategy for navigating the holiday season. What we think we want a month out may be different from what we realize we want as the day grows near. Changing the plan is ok; the key is to develop a strategy that your family can support and follow.

- This type of discussion should be held without distractions so that everyone can focus together. That means holding the meeting in the privacy of your home without visitors. Gather around the kitchen table or in another comfortable part of your home where you can sit face-to-face and really connect without the disruption of phones, devices, television, or other distractions.

- Affirm that all emotions you and your family members share are valid. Support the best you can, regroup, and then move on.

- Look back at other holidays you may have already shared since your loved one died. Briefly share what worked, and what didn't. The key is to quickly revisit and then revise so that the next event will be easier.

- Discuss emotional triggers. In other words, what needs to be avoided, what needs to be included to help avoid those emotional potholes?

- Acknowledge that the grieving process is difficult, normalize the feelings in your family, regroup so that you can learn from what works and what didn't, and then move on.

Special Projects And Activities

- Create a memory collage using photos or magazine cut-outs of things that remind you of your loved one. Laminate your finished collage and use it as a placemat or wall hanging.

- Decorate a photo frame for your loved one's picture and display it prominently.

- Create a "support chain" by linking strips of construction paper with memories of loved ones or other holidays or whatever you decide written on the strips.

- Write memories of special times with your loved ones on scraps of paper. Share them with one another, then place them in an ornament or decorative jar to leave out during the holidays.

- Cook your loved one's favorite meal, and invite someone to share it with you.

- Light a special candle, and create your own ritual. This could be sharing a favorite holiday memory, giving thanks for the blessings in your life, or asking for what you need.

NOTES

GRIEVING MEN, GRIEVING WOMEN

Myth

Women grieve more deeply than men.

Fact

Men grieve as deeply as women, but they often
experience and express loss in a different way.

Just as adults often think children aren't grieving, because childhood
grief doesn't look like adult grief, sometimes women think the men in
their lives aren't grieving. Men and women, adults and children all feel
the sharp, deep pain of the death of a loved one, but they express those
feelings in very different ways.

In western culture, men are often explicitly told not to cry, to think
about something else, to squeeze their eyes shut, to look off into the
distance, to do anything but let a tear fall. Women are freely given
permission to cry, and show painful emotions. When men and women
are together grieving the same loss, it can feel lonely and confusing.
Women often tend to want to talk about what happened, and how
they're feeling about the hard changes in their lives: the missing, the
sadness, the anger and the pain. Men often shy away from talking
about it. Instead, they tend to want to put their feelings into action, to
do something. If they cry, they tend to do so alone. The message that
it's "unmanly" to express the pain of profound loss is taught early in a
boy's life.

Craig's Story

"My mother died when I was 5. She left behind my father and three small children. My dad was crushed by her death, but he never let us see his grief. He soldiered on, and expected everyone around him to do the same. He quickly went back to work, leaving us with a caretaker. When he came home, he never asked how I was doing, and he certainly never shared what he was feeling. I was a boy and I was expected to learn from his stoic example. As a result, this defining event in all our lives was off limits for discussion. Our family took their cue from his behavior. 'Be strong and don't cry. You need to be a man for your father.' It didn't matter that what I needed most was someone to help me understand the fact that my mother was dead, and she was never coming back. My father had walled off his emotions, and I soon learned that I needed to do the same. In the process I became invisible, acutely aware that I was alone in feeling the weight of my mother's loss.

Fast forward many years to the recent death of a dear friend. Betty was a neighbor and the mother of a close childhood friend. After my mother passed away and all the relatives left, she quickly became a second mom to me. It was Betty who helped me to navigate the often confusing years after my father remarried, when I found myself living with a stepmother who had little time or energy to love a child that was not her own. Betty and I kept in close contact, even after I left home for college clear across the county. Though I had seen her just weeks before her death and knew she was failing, I was totally blindsided by the flood of emotions I felt, and tried to squelch, at her funeral.

As I furiously fought back tears, I felt shame and vulnerability that my emotions were visible to others that I had known. Even though I have a loving family to support me, the messages of what it means to be a man haunted me. If I needed to be strong for others, how could I open up to share the burden of grief? Once again, I found myself alone, isolated, and in pain.

In writing this, I know I'm not alone in these feelings. Our culture gives men mixed messages when it comes to death and loss. On the one hand, we expect men to suffer in silence. On the other hand, we judge them harshly as cold, distant and unfeeling when they appear not to be grieving fully. What a bind to be in! It's not surprising that so many men express their grief with action, anger, and addiction."

Maybe you prefer to cry alone, or maybe you want a witness to your pain. Either way, it's important to give yourself permission to be vulnerable. If you don't find intentional ways to express your grief, you can't begin to heal.

For many men, putting feelings into action means creating a project in memory or honor of the person who died. Sometimes it means tearing apart the garage and reorganizing everything. One young man described his feelings in grief group as "jitter-buggy." For him it felt like anxious over-activity, like he didn't know where to land.

One emotion that many men tend to find acceptable to express is anger. Judy Tatelbaum in The Courage to Grieve wrote, "Anger is our protest against that which cannot be changed." For men, it can feel more acceptable to punch a wall because you miss your loved one than to shed a tear. Taught to hide, deny, repress, and avoid their feelings, men learn to fool themselves into believing they can power their way through grief. Eventually, the debt comes due. Cut off from their feelings, it's common for men to shut up and shut down, distancing themselves from their remaining loved ones and their hearts. When this happens, complicated grief can set in, destroying their ability to enjoy life again. That grief may take the form of:

- **Physical symptoms,** such as headaches, fatigue, stomach problems and body aches.

- **Substance abuse,** addictive behavior and/or dependency.

- **Increased accidents.**

- **Chronic depression**, irritability, and withdrawal.

- **Indifference** toward others, insensitivity and workaholism.

Navigating Your Way Through Grief

- Give yourself permission to experience your loss in your own way. Cry or not as you want. It doesn't matter what others think.

- Give yourself time and space to mourn. Don't let others set a timetable for you.

- Allow yourself to slow down and focus on what you need.

- Build on this experience and use it to rebuild your life.

Supporting A Man Who Is Grieving

- Every man experiences grief in his own way. It's okay for men to grieve differently.

- Just because a man is silent doesn't mean he isn't mourning.

- Men tend to think their way through problems. Give them time to work through their feelings.

- Many men prefer time alone in order to heal.

- It's okay for men to feel and express anger, and not to cry. These are typical masculine responses to grief that may help them to heal.

- Be aware of special events and holidays and reach out to let your loved one know he's not alone.

- Gently encourage, but never push your loved one to share his feelings. Telling someone how to grieve will only cause them to shut down emotionally, pushing them further into their pain.

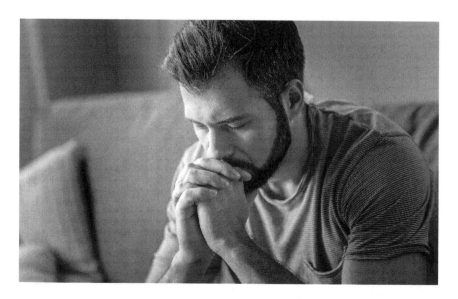

Tune In To What Matters Most

RIGHT THING

- Grief is a unique experience for every man, and the way you grieve may not be what others expect or even what you expected of yourself. However, all men and women need connection and empathy to work through their loss in healthy ways.

- Because of your gender, people may not see you as the bereaved person, but rather look to you to be stoic and strong. Don't confuse grieving with weakness. Find a safe place or someone to share your loss with who isn't afraid of your feelings, and let your grief out. Holding in these strong emotions isn't healthy for you physically or emotionally. Feel the feelings wash over you, and don't worry about what others think.

RIGHT TIME

- When a loved one dies, there are arrangements to be made, children to care for, and other mourners to attend to. It can be easy for men to fall into the support role, swallowing their own feelings in the process. While no man wants to shirk his duties, it's important to give yourself time to grieve. Let go of the mindset that you will focus on yourself after everything and everyone else is taken care of—your emotions and needs are every bit, if not more important to yourself and the wellbeing of your family.

RIGHT WAY

- When men experience loss, they tend to get overlooked. They're expected to be strong, to "suck it up," and get on with things. When others fail to acknowledge their losses, men can feel isolated and misunderstood, and that can cause them to tamp down grief even further. Sharing grief and letting out emotions, however difficult, is crucial to the healing process.

- Consider finding other men to speak with, especially those who have the personal experience or training to understand what you are going through. It can take courage and humility to admit you need help, and to ask for it, but these connections can be some of your strongest sources of support and healing.

NOTES

SUICIDE, HOMICIDE & ACCIDENTAL OVERDOSES

Myth

You protect children by shielding them from the facts.

Fact

Children need to know the truth about how their loved one died.
Present age-appropriate details with care.

Cynthia's Story

Cynthia came to the Grief Center hunched over, shuffling, and wincing as she walked. Her young grandchildren trailed behind her silently with big, round eyes. The family was hurting. Cynthia explained that her daughter had died in a car accident the year before. The truth turned out to be different.

The day she died, Cynthia's daughter visited her children at school and called them out of class, hugged them, and said goodbye. Then she went home and hung herself. Hours after school let out, Cynthia came to pick up her grandchildren, and took them to her house. The kids never returned to the home they had shared with their mother.

Cynthia told everyone that her daughter had died in a car accident. Slowly, a new pattern developed for the family. Little by little, both of the children began to shut down. They stopped talking in school. Her grandson got into a fistfight on the playground, but wouldn't say why or what happened.

A very concerned school counselor called and encouraged Cynthia to attend the Grief Center, but Cynthia was afraid to take the kids to a place where they would talk about their mother's death. Nearly a year later, the counselor was finally able to connect a crying Cynthia with the Grief Center. While the kids were each in their own grief group, listening to others who'd experienced death in their own families, Cynthia was in a group of her own. The first thing she asked her group was if she should tell her grandchildren how their mother had really died.

Over the following months, Cynthia found the words and the strength to tell the children what had really happened to their mom. They seemed to have already known. It wasn't as hard as she had thought. Nearly imperceptibly, the whole family started to shift. Cynthia started walking without pain and standing taller. The kids started to share in group. They practiced talking about their mom and telling their stories. They began to smile. Eventually, they started to laugh again.

Several years after the family closed from group and went on their own way, I ran into the oldest child. She had just started 8th grade and was bubbly with all of the excitement in her life. I asked her how she was doing and she said, "Well, last month was mom's birthday, so we made her favorite dinner, and we told stories about her. We talked about what we missed. We talked about what we wished was different. She was a great mom, but she didn't know how to handle her pain sometimes. Still, we made it a good birthday!"

Giving The Hard News That Someone Has Died

Just as we explain any other death to children, we start by concretely defining what has happened. We always tell the truth in an age-appropriate way, which allows us to build a foundation of trust. To begin with, say that someone has died. For very young children, we have to explain the difference between alive and dead. We have to explain that once someone has died, they cannot breathe, think, walk, talk, or feel. As fundamental as it sounds, it's important to define the language we use like "died" before we introduce our beliefs about afterlife or anything else.

When telling a young person that someone they love has died, take your time. Allow for silence. Allow for questions. It's ok to say "I don't know the answer to that, but I will help you find out."

Telling Kids Someone They Loved Died By Suicide

At the Grief Center we are careful to say "died by suicide" as opposed to "committed suicide." When someone dies by suicide, we say they were hurting so much that this was the only way they knew to stop the pain. They had a very specific kind of illness in the brain—mental illness—and the illness made it impossible for them to think clearly and to get the help they needed.

A death by suicide is sudden. It's unexpected. Everyone is in shock. If you don't say everything you wanted to the first time you talk about the death, you can go back and do it again. It's ok to bring it up. Everyone is thinking about it anyway, even if they try to act like they're not. It's important to emphasize, no matter what the situation, that the special person who died did not choose to leave their loved ones behind, and never intended to hurt them. It's also very important to emphasize that when someone is determined to die by suicide, there is no amount of love that can stop them. To paraphrase Donna Schuurman, Executive Director of The Dougy Center in Portland, Oregon: As we can't love someone out of dying from cancer or a car accident, we can't love someone out of suicide. Mental illness is a powerful illness, and the choice that our loved one made to end their life was beyond our control.

Special Concerns In Surviving A Suicide Death

- **Is it genetic or contagious?** Children who are related to someone who dies by suicide need to be reassured that this is not their fate as well. It's ok to say, "They had a very serious mental illness, but this does not mean anyone else in our family has to die this way. There are doctors and medications that can help. The key is to talk about it, to ask for help, and to know that dying isn't the only solution."

- **Stigma.** Most people will not understand the many powerful emotions and questions that accompany a loved one's suicide. Try to connect with others who've survived the suicide of a loved one. Support groups and internet sites abound with people who have walked this path before you. There are numerous detailed, helpful books on the subject.

- **Faith.** Most deaths challenge our faith. Many Catholics, for example, believe that if someone took their own life, their souls are doomed for eternity. The 1994 publication of the Catechism of the Catholic Church says the suicide breaks the natural path of life, but that the church will pray for those who died by suicide.

- **Guilt.** Survivors of a loved one's suicide may ask themselves what they could have done to save them. The answer is: nothing. If someone is determined to die by suicide, they will. Connect with other survivors who understand this pain. Children will often feel they did or said something that caused their loved one to die. Bring this up directly and remind them that they are not responsible for their loved one's death.

Telling Kids Someone Died By Homicide

The fact is that someone important in this child's life is gone. That is the first and foremost issue. The "how" it happened can be given in small doses appropriate for the child's age and understanding.

When someone we love dies, and it is the fault of someone else's actions—be it accidental or with intent—it can be easy to focus the anger, rage, and hurt toward the other person. Seeking vengeance or justice can occupy so much of the survivors' lives that they lose focus on the loved ones remaining. Sitting in a courtroom and hearing the details of the deceased's last moments, even watching the person responsible receive a severe punishment, won't make the pain go away. That can be another great loss, and very hard to accept.

Special Concerns Following A Homicide

- **Stigma.** Many people believe that if someone is murdered, they must have had it coming to them.

- **Fear.** The reality that someone we love can die at the hand of someone else can make the world feel like a very scary place. It's important to emphasize all that is done and will be done to keep the other people in the family safe. Homicide, as much as we hear about it in the media, and even when it occurs in our own families, is a relatively rare way to die. Children who experience any manner of death are hypersensitive to the fact that everyone they love can and will die eventually. Reassure them that there will always be someone to take care of them.

- **Revenge.** Father Richard Rohr once said, "Pain that is not transformed, is transmitted." The idea that hurting the person who hurt us will somehow mitigate our pain is an old and outdated idea. It does not work. We have to mourn the person we lost and reinvest in life.

- **Guilt.** Survivors of a loved one's homicide can replay the moments before their lives changed forever and see many things they could or should have done. Nothing can change what happened. We can change how we go forward into each new day. Children will often feel they did or said something that caused their loved one to die. Bring this up directly. Remind them that they are not responsible for their loved one's death.

- **Media.** If the circumstances surrounding the death of your loved one are played out on the nightly news, in the paper, or in social media, it can feel inescapable. Often media accounts get the details wrong. Sometimes, they portray the person we loved in an unflattering light. Sometimes, they invade your space. It is ok to say no to reporters. You can't correct all the misinformation in the world, but you can let the young people in your life know that it's out there. There will be rumors, stories, and questions. We don't have to respond to them unless we feel ready.

Telling Kids Someone Died By Accidental Overdose

Please take a moment to read through the sections on suicide and homicide. Death by accidental overdose seems to lie between those two experiences. An accidental overdose can occur when someone we love has struggled with addiction, and sometimes it can occur because someone just mixed the wrong medications. Sometimes we don't know how it happened. Special concerns in an overdose death:

- **Addiction.** If substance abuse runs in the family, talk about it early and often. Talk about avoiding ever trying the addictive substances. If kids are worried about substance abuse, talk about how to get help. Reaching out to a trusted adult (parent of a friend, teacher, coach, or school counselor) is always a good place to start.

- **Guilt.** The "would have, should haves" can take over. Nothing can change what happened. We can change how we go forward into each new day. Children will often feel they did or said something that caused their loved one to die. Bring this up directly and remind them that they are not responsible for their loved one's death.

In all of these sudden losses, there isn't time to say goodbye. That can be an ongoing struggle for survivors. Your conversation with your loved one was cut short. When you are ready, and it may be sometime after the memorial or funeral services, you can take time out to say a special goodbye. There are many ways to include the young people in the family. Write a message on a balloon and send it up into the sky. Write messages on paper and burn them in a special fire. Talk to a picture or other tangible representation of your loved one. Just because you do it once, doesn't mean you can't do it again if you need to.

Tune In To What Matters Most

RIGHT THING

- When someone close to you dies by suicide, homicide, or overdose, it can be difficult to comprehend. Tune into your emotions as a first step toward understanding them.

- You may experience feelings of shock, anger and guilt. Not only have you lost a loved one, but the circumstances and trauma makes coping much more difficult.

- There is no making sense of why someone would take their life, murder your loved one, or how things could come to an overdose. In the meantime, know that there is nothing wrong with you and get help to support your healing.

RIGHT TIME

- Shock is a common reaction to death, especially one that is sudden and unexpected. You may feel numb for a few days, a few weeks, or even longer.

- Take some time to be alone if that's what you want and need, but be careful not to isolate yourself. Return to your own life and routine as soon as you feel ready.

RIGHT WAY

- The right way to handle this type of loss is by giving yourself permission to feel whatever feelings you have and to process them in whatever way works for you.

- These feelings may overwhelm you at first, but trust that you can handle and move past them with time. Try to understand and accept that your emotions are normal, healthy and a painful but necessary part of the healing process.

NOTES

FINDING A NEW WAY TO FEEL NORMAL AGAIN

Myth

Time heals all wounds.

Fact

"The medicine of time, taken by itself, is not a cure. Time is neutral. What helps is what you do with time." Rabbi Earl Grollman

Mark's Story

"When my wife died, I was a trainwreck. We had three boys. They were 12, 8, and 6. She was sick for a year. We knew she was going to die. It was just crazy. They said goodbye, and then it was like everything fell apart. What had kept us going—being there through her illness—just stopped when she did.

The oldest was drawing pictures of shooting himself. The middle one was hiding under his desk at school, holding onto a blanket she had given him. The youngest was getting picked on at school. He was vulnerable. He was a target. I couldn't sleep, and I didn't want to cry in front my sons because I'm a man, and I didn't think that was an ok example to set. We were lost, numb. We found our way to the Grief Center. After the first night, I asked the boys "What'd you think of it?" and they said 'They're like us, dad. They're just like us.' I was in a group of women who'd lost their husbands, and we learned about our grief together. The kids would play, they'd share their story, and slowly we started to be able to talk about her in our groups and then together. A few years have passed now. The Grief Center got us to the point....we live our life. We love like nobody's business. We enjoy each day."

The moment you hear the news that someone you love has died, your world is never the same. The first few days streak by with arrangements to be made, well-wishers visiting, a kind of surreal numbness settles over everything. Some of us respond by diving into the busyness, like a spinning top. If we stop spinning, we fall down. Others retreat from the world, denying the reality of the loss, pushing away the horrible decisions and tasks that come along with death.

It's difficult to imagine ever feeling normal or ok again. In a way—you won't. You'll be forever shaped by this experience. Profound grief changes us. Part of our work is to recognize those changes, and to become ok with them.

There are many who have walked this grief journey before you. They know the immediate, wrenching pain of the loss. They know the slow ache that never fully subsides. They know that even as years pass, the process of reconciling the loss of a loved one into our ongoing lives can often feel like resignation.

They know it's so hard to believe now, but there is a future for you and your family. It can even be a beautiful future.

We asked several families who've been through the death of a partner or child to share their thoughts. This is what they had to say:

Things I Want Newly Bereaved Parents To Know:

- You are going to survive this.

- You learn to love a whole lot better, stronger, differently.

- You learn not to take anyone for granted. You learn the value of your loved ones. You learn that life is not guaranteed.

- You get accustomed to being uncomfortable.

- You do some nutty things when you're grieving. Your kids do some nutty things, too. Meet them at the place they are.

- You have to learn what your "new normal" is and remember you're not setting the table for the same number of people anymore.

- You need to tell the kids, "It's ok if I cry. I'm crying because I loved them. You are not making me cry."

The First Year After My Loved One Died

- I felt like a walking ghost.

- I don't know how I got through it.

- Grieving isn't done in one year, it's not done in three, nor in six.

- I have a need to keep my life "neater." I think about what I will leave behind if I die suddenly.

- We talk about kids regressing, but even adults revert to comforting or immature behaviors.

- Pay attention to your own intuition about what is right for your kids/family.

At the Grief Center, we sometimes encounter children, teens, and even adults who have identified so closely with the pain of loss that they become accustomed to dwelling in their own personal shadow. They may feel guilt or shame if they were to laugh or enjoy themselves, as if experiencing life more fully again would disrespect the memory of the person who died, or dishonor their own experience of grieving that loss.

In A Grief Observed, C.S. Lewis wrote, "Getting over a painful experience is much like crossing the monkey bars—you have to let go at some point to move forward."

Not sure how to let go to move forward? We can learn from the youngest children in our families. They experience the pain of the loss, they pause, recognize, feel the hard feelings, and then they continue on. This may happen a few times a day, or a few times a week. Eventually, the times between those sharp points of painful grief will expand, and fill with what has become your new life. It takes care, it takes honoring those experiences, and it takes the courage to let them go. Like everything else on this journey, it will happen at a different pace for the different members of your family.

A young mother of three children ages 2, 6, and 10 was visited by police chaplains bearing the news that her husband had just been killed in a motorcycle accident. She brought her family to the Children's Grief Center, and they were able to participate in peer support groups, share their stories, and learn from others. Over the course of a few years, the children grew up, and they grew strong. They were able to talk about their father clearly with joy and with sadness, to recognize the experience of his loss in their lives and to move in and out of the hard feelings that accompany grief. Eventually, their mother fell in love again, with a wonderful man. Speaking publicly about their experience for the first time she said, "The Grief Center allowed us to step into the life that was waiting for us."

Whether or not you have a place like the Children's Grief Center in your town, you have a community. You have these stories. You have resources in the back of this book where you can connect virtually to others who share experiences like yours. You are not alone. You are "stronger than you believe and braver than you think" to paraphrase that great sage, Winnie the Pooh. There is a life waiting for you. We promise.

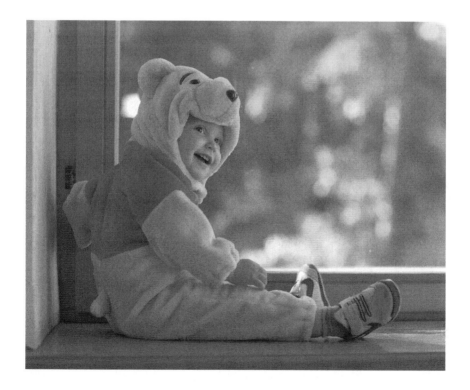

Internet Resources

Hello Grief. An online support community for teens: **hellogrief.org**

National Alliance for Grieving Children: **childrengrieve.org**

The Children's Grief Center of New Mexico: **childrensgrief.org**

Support for Cancer's Widowers: **singlefathersduetocancer.org**

Comfort Zone Camp, a national camp for grieving
young people: **comfortzonecamp.org**

The Compassionate Friends, a support group of parents
who have lost children: **compassionatefriends.org**

The Dougy Center: **dougy.org**

Grief-related Training: **learningaboutloss.com**

Suicide loss: **suicidefindinghope.com**

Grief & Loss Books For Young Children

Saying Goodbye to Daddy, Judith Vigna

The Tenth Good Thing About Barney, Judith Viorst

Tell The Paper, A Centering Corporation Resource

The Fall of Freddie the Leaf, Leo Buscalgia

Healing Your Grieving Heart: 100 Practical Ideas for Kids, Alan Wolfelt

Lifetimes: the Beautiful way to Explain Death to Children
Bryan Mellonie and Robert Ingpen

When Someone Very Special Dies, Children Can
Learn To Cope With Grief, Marge Heegaard

Badger's Parting Gifts, Susan Varley

About The Authors

Jade Richardson Bock has worked in the grief and loss community since 2003. In 2019 she founded **learningaboutloss.com**, a collection of resources and expert advice on navigating life after death.

As the Executive Director of the Children's Grief Center of New Mexico for over a decade, Ms. Bock spent hundreds of hours facilitating grief support groups with children, teens, young adults, and their adult caregivers. Her most meaningful and poignant education on how families grieve began at age 17 when her father was killed in a plane crash.

Dr. Craig Pierce is the CEO of Southwest Family Guidance and Institute. He is a Clinical Fellow with the American Association of Marriage and Family Therapy and a Fellow and board certified PTSD Clinician by APA.

Dr. Pierce and his team at the Institute developed the work of Thriving Kids and Thriving Students, which support families and schools in helping children thrive in spite of incredible challenges.

His grief work with children and families is inspired by his own experience with childhood loss. **swfamily.com**

Children's Grief Center

The Children's Grief Center of New Mexico provides free bereavement support services for children ages 5–25 and their caregivers following the death of a loved one. Nationwide, 1 in 14 children will lose a parent or sibling before the age of 18. In New Mexico, the incidence is even higher, with 1 in 10 children becoming significantly bereaved before reaching adulthood.

Children need proper support for their grief and are often the quiet or forgotten grievers. Bereaved children are at a higher risk for depression, anxiety, substance abuse, problems in school, and criminal activity. The Children's Grief Center provides a place where children discover there are others like them, the death was not their fault, and their loved one did not want to leave them. They learn age appropriate ways to process their grief and identify healthy coping techniques that increase resiliency throughout their lives. This important work helps mitigate a lifetime of struggles that can result from unresolved grief. Children, teens, young adults, and their caregivers gain vital hope for the future at the Children's Grief Center of New Mexico.

When someone dies you don't get through it by forgetting;
you get through it by remembering.

The Children's Grief Center is supported entirely through donations
and leverages a large volunteer pool to provide these programs.
All proceeds from this book go to the Children's Grief Center
to support these efforts. Donations can be made online at

childrensgrief.org

More information and volunteer opportunities can be found
on our website or by calling (505) 323 0478.

Thank you for your support!

Made in the USA
Middletown, DE
17 May 2022

65860891R00053